Two-Minute Brainteasers

ALAN STILLSON

Official Mensa
Puzzle Book

Sterling Publishing Co., Inc.
New York

For Gail
and our ever-supportive family

Edited by Jeanette Green
Designed by Karen Minster
Proofread by Lisa J. Smith

Library of Congress Cataloging-in-Publication Data

Stillson, Alan.
  Two-minute brainteasers / Alan Stillson.
  p. cm. – (Official Mensa puzzle book)
  Includes index.
  ISBN 1-4027-1827-6
  1. Word games. I. Title. II. Series.

GV1507.W8S795 2005
796.734–dc22

                    2005013729

10   9   8   7   6   5   4   3   2   1

Published by Sterling Publishing Co., Inc.
387 Park Avenue South, New York, NY 10016.
© 2005 by Alan Stillson.
Distributed in Canada by Sterling Publishing,
c/o Canadian Manda Group, 165 Dufferin Street,
Toronto, Ontario, Canada M6K 3H6.
Distributed in Great Britain by Chrysalis Books Group PLC. The Chrysalis
Building, Bramley Road, London W10 6SP, England.
Distributed in Australia by Capricorn Link (Australia) Pty. Ltd., P.O. Box 704,
Windsor, NSW 2756, Australia
Printed in China
All rights reserved

ISBN 1-4027-1827-6

For information about custom editions, special sales, premium and corporate
purchases, please contact Sterling Special Sales Department at 800-805-5489 or
specialsales@sterlingpub.com.

CONTENTS

Introduction   5
American Mensa Puzzle-Testing Panel   6

Part I   Quick Word Puzzles   7

1   Q Puzzles   8
2   Z Puzzles   9
3   J Puzzles   10
4   X Puzzles   11
5   K Puzzles   12
6   Movies–the 1980s   13
7   Non-Repeaters   15
8   Holiday Season Letter Zappers   17
9   Words of the Presidents   19
10   Add-a-Letter   21
11   Drop Letters   23
12   Add-On Words   25

Part II   Something in Common   27

1   Miscellany   29
2   Same-Size Words   35
3   Names & Places   41
4   Name Shuffles (Kid-Friendly Bonus)   48

Part III   Special Days   49

1   Valentine's Day   50
2   St. Patrick's Day   51
3   Independence Day   52
4   Labor Day   53
5   Columbus Day   54

Part IV Celebrities   55

1   Singers   56
2   Actors   58
3   Athletes   60
4   Sam, Dan & Ron Are Hiding (Kid-Friendly Bonus)   62

Part V Hidden Things   63

1   Hidden Math Words   64
2   Hidden Automobile Models   65
3   Hidden Authors   66

Part VI Synanagrams   67

1   States & Provinces in North America   68
2   Chemical Elements   69
3   Professional Sports Teams   70
4   National Parks   71
5   Dog & Cat Breeds   72
6   Incomplete Alphabet Messages (Bonus)   73

Answers   75

PART I   Quick Word Puzzles   76
PART II   Something in Common   81
PART III   Special Days   84
PART IV   Celebrities   86
PART V   Hidden Things   88
PART VI   Synanagrams   90

Index to Puzzles   93
Index to Answers   94

What Is Mensa?   95

INTRODUCTION

Two-Minute Brainteasers completes a trilogy of Mensa brainteaser books featuring short, thematic no-pencil word puzzles. If you've enjoyed the first two official Mensa puzzle books, *One-Minute Brainteasers* (Sterling, 2001) and *Ninety-Second Brainteasers* (Sterling, 2003), you'll find some familiar themes as well as new ones. We've even introduced a few kid-friendly puzzles so that the whole family can share in the fun.

You'll have over 450 new puzzles to work. Most puzzles can be solved within two minutes, which allows you, the busy thinker, to control and time your mental workouts. Each puzzle can be solved independently of the others. That means that you can begin and end wherever and whenever you wish. When you're ready for more mental exercise, simply pick up where you left off or venture into a new patch of questions.

If you're like me, with trivia questions you either remember the fact or you do not. Brainteasers, however, coax a little thought and tease you into constructs or concepts of your own. We like to think of them as breezy mental gymnastics that are great fun.

How easy or hard are these puzzles? Our American Mensa puzzle panel tested each brainteaser. You can compare your results with those of our panel, which solved about 55% of the puzzles correctly. Of course, results varied from one group of puzzles to another.

Naturally, some puzzles may have alternative solutions that we didn't think of. If so, kudos to you! Evaluate your results accordingly.

Puzzles are found in six parts or categories: "Quick Word Puzzles," "Something in Common," "Special Days," "Celebrities," "Hidden Things," and "Synanagrams." You'll find the kid-friendly questions after the more challenging adult puzzles in Parts II and IV. A bonus section, "Incomplete Alphabet Messages," appears after the synanagrams.

Ready to rev up your mental engine? Here's your green light. Thirty-five members of American Mensa, Ltd., people who have IQs in the top 2% of the American population, volunteered for the testing panel for *Two-Minute Brainteasers*. They received the puzzles by e-mail with instructions to take no more than about two minutes per puzzle. When they sent back their answers, we tabulated the results, rounding off the percentage of correct answers to the nearest 5% for each group of puzzles and for the whole book.

American Mensa Puzzle-Testing Panel

I'd like to give special thanks to members of the Mensa puzzle-testing panel for this book: Dean A. Beers; Bob Berreth; Nancy Berringer; Walt Bodner; Howard Bryks; Jody Carlson; Karen J. Cooper; Mo Demers; Chris Dudlak; Jonathan Elliott; Jay French; Ann M. Garbler; Jennifer W. Gittins; Louis Grimm; Eric Holmquist; G. Christom Larsin; Dennis Littlefield; Vince Lobuzzetta; Ron Ludwig; Joann Ayers Lynn; Karen Marchisotto; Sean McAuliffe; Raymond McCauley; Dr. Robert J. Meier; Chuck Murphy; Dave Murphy; Brett Radlicki; Ginger Rowe; Bill Siderski (with help from his 12-year-old son, Kyle); Barbara A. Steiner; Pat Stenger; Timothy J. Sullivan; Bethany Thivierge; Mitchell I. Weisberg; and Markell Raphaelson West.

I tip my hat to Jonathan Elliott and Markell Raphaelson West for offering extensive editorial suggestions.

About the Author

Alan Stillson's puzzles have appeared in *American Way*, the American Airlines in-flight magazine. He is puzzle editor for Greater Los Angeles Mensa and provides puzzles to local Mensa publications throughout the United States and Canada. His official American Mensa puzzle books, *One-Minute Brainteasers* (Sterling, 2001), *Ninety Second Brainteasers* (Sterling, 2003), *The Mensa Genius ABC Quiz Book*, and *Match Wits with Mensa: The Complete Quiz Book,* co-authored with Marvin Grosswirth and Dr. Abbie Salny, continue to delight readers. Other puzzle books include *Middle School Word Puzzles* and *What's Your CQ?* His puzzles have been reviewed in *People* magazine. Mr. Stillson is a member of Mensa, the National Puzzlers' League, and the National Scrabble Association.

Part I

QUICK WORD PUZZLES

Q Puzzles

Words with the letter *Q* are rare, and short sentences with two *Q*-words are rarer. For example, "A Q _ _ _ _ _ _ at a meeting is a _ _ _ _ _ Q _ _ _ _ _ _ _ for voting on motions" would make sense with *quorum* and *prerequisite*.

Fill in the blanks so that the *Q* words make sense in the context.

1. _ _ _ Q _ _ _ _ _ _ _ was known for his brutality during the Spanish _ _ Q _ _ _ _ _ _ _ _ _ .

2. Q _ _ _ _ _ _ and _ _ _ Q are French digits.

3. They encountered a _ Q _ _ _ _ _ _ _ of soldiers from the _ _ _ Q _ Republican Guard.

4. The politician went into a fit of _ _ Q _ _ _ every time a reporter _ _ _ Q _ _ _ _ _ him.

5. Some people attributed her _ _ Q _ _ _ _ _ _ _ _ ways to feminine _ _ _ _ _ Q _ _ .

6. The lawyer could have won an _ _ Q _ _ _ _ _ _ _ for the _ _ _ Q _ _ _ _ de Sade.

7. Is it possible to substitute Q _ _ _ _ _ _ for lobster in a _ _ _ Q _ _ ?

8. The _ _ _ Q _ _ _ _ _ transmits malaria, which can be treated with Q _ _ _ _ _ _ _ .

9. The patisserie featured _ _ _ Q _ _ _ monsieur and four varieties of Q _ _ _ _ _ _ .

10. Using the Q _ _ _ _ _ _ _ _ _ _ formula involves finding a _ Q _ _ _ _ _ root.

Answers are on page 76.

MENSA SCORING

Average Mensa Score:	65%

Z Puzzles

Words with the letter *Z* are rare, and short sentences with two *Z*-words are rarer. For example, "The jeweler carefully placed the cubic Z _ _ _ _ _ _ _ _ _ into the _ _ Z _ _ " would make sense with the words *zirconium* and *bezel*.

Fill in the blanks so that the two *Z*-words make sense.

1. Z _ _ _ doesn't _ _ _ _ _ Z _ as easily as iron.

2. The Varig flight stopped in _ _ _ _ Z _ and terminated in _ _ _ Z _ _ .

3. At the Greek restaurant, they enjoyed a glass of _ _ Z _ and some _ _ _ Z _ _ _ _ music.

4. This Tin _ _ Z Z _ was once owned by _ _ Z Z _ Dean.

5. W. A. _ _ Z _ _ _ was born in _ _ _ Z _ _ _ _ .

6. Smog results when _ Z _ _ _ forms a _ _ Z _ mist.

7. It's unlikely that _ _ _ Z _ ever lived in a Z _ _ with other primates.

8. The _ Z _ _ of Russia had never encountered a religious Z _ _ _ _ _ .

9. The waiter recommended a white Z _ _ _ _ _ _ _ _ _ to drink with the _ _ _ _ _ _ Z _ _ .

10. The Judy who met the _ _ Z _ _ _ named her daughter _ _ Z _

Answers are on page 76.

MENSA SCORING

Average Mensa Score:	60%

9

J Puzzles

Words with the letter *J* are rare, and short sentences with two *J*-words are rarer. For example, "The ship with the J _ _ _ _ _ Roger fired at the ship with the Union J _ _ _ _ " would make sense with the words *Jolly* and *Jack.*

Fill in the blanks so that the two *J*-words make sense.

1. The _ _J_ _ _ _ _ _ of the people living in Amman, J _ _ _ _ _ _, are Muslims.

2. J _ _ _ is practiced at a _ _J_.

3. The wine store had everything from a J _ _ _ _ _ _ _ of French champagne to a quart of Spanish _ _ _J_.

4. Did the citizens of El Paso _ _J_ _ _ a proposal to build another border crossing into J _ _ _ _ _ ?

5. They saw the film _ _*J*_ _ _ *Game* at a small theater in J _ _ _ _ _ _ Hole.

6. The _ _ _J_ player tried to _ _J_ _ _ to a different tuning.

7. The price of pure J _J _ _ _ oil can be J _ _ _ _ _ _.

8. The meat was seasoned with _ _J_ _ mustard and _ _ _J_ _ _ _.

9. She liked watching reruns of J _ _ _ _ J _ _ _.

10. Flotsam and J _ _ _ _ _ were polluting the _J_ _ _.

Answers are on page 76.

X Puzzles

Words with the letter *X* are rare, and short sentences with two *X*-words are rarer. For example, "The trip to Egypt included stops at the _ _ _ _ _ X and at _ _ _ X _ _ _ _ _ _ "
would make sense with *Sphinx* and *Alexandria*.

Fill in the blanks so that the two *X*-words make sense.

1. An increase in the number of _ _ X _ _ _ _ can improve the quality of graphics
   _ X _ _ _ _ _ _ _ _ _ _ _ _ _ .

2. The _ _ _ _ X of the matter is that the supervisor blatantly made a _ _ X _ _ _ _ remark.

3. The _ X _ _ _ _ _ _ _ _ survived a
   _ _ _ X _ vote.

4. _ _ _ _ _ X treatments are risky and may be too
   _ _ X _ _ for some people.

5. She created a _ _ _ _ _ _ X using Microsoft
   _ X _ _ _ .

6. An _ X _ _ _ _ _ _ _ _ _ _ _ _ _
   _ _ X _ _ _ _ _ led the rowing team.

7. He took an _ X _ _ _ _ _ _ train from Brooklyn to the _ _ _ _ X .

8. _ _ X _ _ _ _ is about three hundred miles southeast of _ _ X _ _ _ City.

9. The lab technician wore _ _ _ _ _ X gloves when handling hydrogen _ _ _ _ X _ _ _ .

10. The Monopoly player had to pay
    _ _ X _ _ _ _ _ _ X.

Answers are on page 76.

MENSA SCORING

Average Mensa Score:	75%

K Puzzles

Words with the letter *K* are rare, and short sentences with two *K*-words are rarer. For example, "The hammer and _ _ _ K _ _ once flew over K _ _ _ " would make sense with the words *sickle* and *Kiev*.

Fill in the blanks so that the two *K*-words make sense.

1. Some employees have a   K _ _ _ K   for
K _ _ _ _ _ _ _ _ _   to their bosses.

2. It's not good business sense to sell a   _ K _ _ _
of wool for a   _ _ _ K _ _.

3. The snowmobile crossed the   K _ _ _ _ _ K _
at   _ _ _ _ K _ _ _ K   speed.

4. Pat Riley once coached the   _ _ K _ _ _ _   and the
K _ _ _ K _ .

5. The student was expelled for carrying a   K _ _ _ _ _
in his   _ _ _ K _ _ _ K .

6. Three consecutive   _ _ _ _ K _ _   is called a
_ _ _ K _ _ .

7. For many years, Massachusetts has been served by
Senators   K _ _ _ _ _ _ _   and   K _ _ _ _ _ .

8. He ordered a   K _ _ _ K _ _ _ _ _   with
_ _ _ _ _ K _ _ _ _ .

9. The Bush home in   K _ _ _ _ _ _ _ _ K _ _ _ _
got   _ _ _ _ K _ _ _ _   by snow.

10. The   _ _ _ K K _ _ _ _ _ _
_ _ K _ _ _ _ _ _ _ _ _   the errors.

Answers are on page 77.

MENSA SCORING	
Average Mensa Score:	70%

Movies—the 1980s

The Letter Monster has been devouring the middle letters from titles of 1980s movies. For example, *Good Morning, Vietnam* (1988), starring Robin Williams, has become

G _ _ D M _ _ _ _ _ _ G, V _ _ _ _ _ M.

Find the original titles of these movies.

1. S _ _ _ _ _ _ _ _ O (1985), starring Kevin Kline, Kevin Costner, and Danny Glover

2. A _ _ _ _ _ _ _ C C _ _ Y (1980), starring Burt Lancaster and Susan Sarandon

3. D _ _ _ Y R _ _ _ _ N S _ _ _ _ _ _ _ _ _ S (1988), starring Steve Martin and Michael Caine

4. A _ _ _ _ _ _ _ N G _ _ _ _ O (1980), starring Richard Gere

5. S _ _ _ _ _ _ _ E (1983), starring Al Pacino

6. N _ _ _ _ _ _ _ _ S (1981), starring John Belushi and Dan Aykroyd

7. W _ _ _ D S _ _ _ _ _ _ E (1985), starring Anthony Michael Hall and Kelly LeBrock

8. B _ _ _ _ _ _ _ Y D _ _ _ _ Y R _ _ E (1984), starring Woody Allen and Mia Farrow

9. G _ _ _ Y P _ _ K (1983), starring William Hurt

10. T _ _ _ _ _ _ G P _ _ _ _ S (1983), starring Eddie Murphy and Dan Aykroyd

Answers are on page 77.

11. *P* _ _ _ _ _ *E*   *B* _ _ _ _ _ _ *N*   (1980),
starring Goldie Hawn and Eileen Brennan

12. *L* _ _ _ _ _ *L*   *W* _ _ _ _ *N*   (1987),
starring Mel Gibson and Danny Glover

13. *C* _ _ _ _ _ _ _ _ _ *K*   (1980),
starring Chevy Chase and Bill Murray

14. *O* _ _ _ _ _ _ _ *Y*   *P* _ _ _ _ *E*   (1989),
starring Donald Sutherland and Mary Tyler Moore

15. *H* _ _ _ _ _ _ _ _ *Y*   (1988),
starring Ricki Lake

16. *T* _ *E*   *V* _ _ _ _ _ *T*   (1982),
starring Paul Newman

17. *J* _ _ _ _ *D*   *E* _ _ *E*   (1985),
starring Glenn Close and Jeff Bridges

18. *T* _ *E*   *F* _ _ _ _ *H*   *P* _ _ _ _ _ _ *L*   (1987),
starring Michael Caine and Pierce Brosnan

19. *R* _ _ _ *Y*   *B* _ _ _ _ _ _ *S*   (1983),
starring Tom Cruise

20. *E* _ _ _ _ _ *E*   *P* _ _ _ _ _ _ _ *E*   (1987),
starring Nick Nolte

Answers are on page 77.

Non-Repeaters

Non-repeaters (also called non-pattern words, isograms, order one isograms, and heterograms) are words where none of the letters repeat. In these puzzles, the first letter of the missing word and the blanks are given. For example, the sentence, "Some medications are administered with a
H _ _ _ _ _ _ _ _ _ _ needle" can be completed with *hypodermic,* a word with no repeated letters.

Fill in the missing letters to form sensible sentences with non-repeaters.

1. The   R _ _ _ _ _ _ _ _ _ _   of the game must wait until the rain stops.

2. The senator fought for the   A _ _ _ _ _ _ _ _ _ _ _ of unfair taxes.

3. Many singles are judged on looks and
P _ _ _ _ _ _ _ _ _ _ _ .

4. The scientist was   F _ _ _ _ _ _ _ _ _ _ a new hypothesis.

5. She made her fortune in land
S _ _ _ _ _ _ _ _ _ _ .

6. Some lawyers always try   O _ _ _ _ _ _ _ _ _ _ the truth.

7. The verb was not   C _ _ _ _ _ _ _ _ _ _ correctly.

8. A   J _ _ _ _ _ _ _ _ _ _   major is expected to be a good speller.

9. Relationships between the countries were finally
N _ _ _ _ _ _ _ _ _ .

10. The coffee is   P _ _ _ _ _ _ _ _ _ _ _ .

Answers are on page 78.

11. The job was finished by his
S _ _ _ _ _ _ _ _ _ _ _ .

12. Pool water is usually   C _ _ _ _ _ _ _ _ _ _ _ .

13. Inflation is   P _ _ _ _ _ _ _ _ _ _ _
to economic growth.

14. Very few people are   A _ _ _ _ _ _ _ _ _ _ _ _ .

15. Some people work better with
B _ _ _ _ _ _ _ _ _ _   music.

16. Some people have had the   M _ _ _ _ _ _ _ _ _ _
of being swindled.

17. Many people   S _ _ _ _ _ _ _ _ _ _   with the
underdog.

18. S _ _ _ _ _ _ _ _ _ _   anger can cause illness.

19. Original songs are   C _ _ _ _ _ _ _ _ _ _ _ _ _ .

20. A quack is not   A _ _ _ _ _ _ _ _ _ _
to practice medicine.

Answers are on page 78.

Holiday Season Letter Zappers

Words, names, and phrases relating to the holiday season (Thanksgiving through New Year's Day) may be found by zapping a few letters in an unrelated phrase. For example, EACH WRIST MASHED can be changed into CHRISTMAS by zapping 6 letters: ~~EA~~CH ~~WR~~IST MAS~~HED~~. The remaining letters will be in the right order.

Find the holiday season word, name, or phrase by doing these letter zappers.

1. NOW READ THIS – zap 5 letters

2. GNATS LIVE IN STY – zap 6 letters

3. SILLY DENT IN FLIGHT – zap 6 letters

4. AMID STALE TOKENS – zap 6 letters

5. SHOO FLY TINS FAINT – zap 6 letters

6. COVER ANOTHER DRIVER – zap 6 letters

7. MY PULLET IS DEAR – zap 6 letters

8. BEASTS HEALED THEM – zap 7 letters

9. PINK WANTS ZAPPA – zap 7 letters

10. CLINT TILED RED HUMMER BODY – zap 7 letters

Answers are on page 78.

8

11. SPRINT FACE OFF PREFACE – zap 7 letters

12. THE CREEP WISHES A MENU – zap 7 letters

13. FROGS TRY THEM AS NO WORM CAN –
zap 7 letters

14. SAVING THE NICE SHOP LAST – zap 8 letters

15. SPUR MAP MAKING SPICE – zap 8 letters

16. FELINE ZONE SAVING DREAD – zap 9 letters

17. HEMAN DUKES OKAY HIM – zap 10 letters

18. CAN BUILD PLAYING EASY ONE –
zap 10 letters

19. STEAMY SONGS AGREEABLE THINGS –
zap 10 letters

20. PLEASANT ACTORS PLAY US – zap 10 letters

Answers are on page 78.

Answers are on page 78.

MENSA SCORING

Average Mensa Score:	60%

Words of the Presidents

In a popular word game, you can write out the first and last names of U.S. Presidents and form as many words as you can from the letters. For example, you can use the letters in Abraham Lincoln's name to make such words as *barn, nail,* and *baronial.* However, *barn* could also have been made from Benjamin Harrison's name and *nail* could also have been made from Franklin Roosevelt's name, but *baronial* can only be made from the letters in Honest Abe's name.

Find the only U.S. President whose letters in the first and last name (no middle name) can be used to make the given words.

1. rewarding

2. pricklier

3. bravura

4. stress

5. honked

6. million

7. filial

8. gala

9. brother

10. showering

Answers are on page 79.

11. gusher

12. festival

13. amassed

14. foraged

15. revolted

16. streamer

17. joys

18. engaging

19. ax

20. revealed

Answers are on page 79.

MENSA SCORING

Average Mensa Score:	75%

Add-a-Letter

We live in a world full of popular first-letter designations (initials) designed to save time. Right now there might be a CD made by a VIP playing in your GM car. In these puzzles, the idea is to add a letter at the end of the first designation to make a new one. For example, going from "by the way" to "pressure measure" is PS to PSI.

Find these add-a-letter designations.

1. Space alien to piece of airport datum

2. Degenerative disease to tax specialist

3. A medium to a New Deal project

4. Law degree to a group founded by Meir Kahane

5. British public servant to fuel efficiency

6. Wandering tabby to 24 for 6 and 8, for example

7. Home for some Dalmatians to drug regulator

8. Junior college degree to driving club

9. Advanced degree to questionable seasoning ingredient

10. Precinct tenant to handheld computer

Answers are on page 79.

Add-a-Letter

11. Radio choice to Rambler maker

12. Gehrig's territory to Gehrig's disease

13. Goal of physics undergraduate to prepared people

14. Inoffensive to road through Malibu

15. 109, for one, to Harper Valley, for one

16. Popular rating to Tiger's territory

17. Prosecutor to female blue-blood group

18. Trucker's tool to network choice

19. Acidity to highest degree

20. Ultimate degree in ministry to infamous pesticide

Answers are on page 79.

Drop Letters

A sentence can be completed sensibly by finding two words where the second word is created by dropping one or more consecutive letters from the first word. In these puzzles, at least two letters will be preserved from the beginning and end of the first word. The letter counts of both missing words are provided as a clue. Here's an example. "_____ (7 letters) to protect yourself from a snake's _____ (4 letters) can be a fatal mistake" makes sense with FAILING and FANG. Note that the first two letters (FA) and the last two letters (NG) of FAILING were preserved and the middle letters were dropped.

Find the pair of words to solve these puzzles.

1. For some actresses, playing a _____ (8 letters) blonde can be a _____ (4 letters) role.

2. Detectable amounts of _____ (9 letters) inside a home may be caused by _____ (5 letters).

3. Making a false _____ (10 letters) could result in legal _____ (6 letters).

4. A _____ (7 letters) person might _____ (4 letters) away the belongings of a homeless child.

5. The politician's efforts were not _____ (9 letters) to much _____ (5 letters) younger voters.

6. The choir was singing a _____ (9 letters) while walking down a _____ (6 letters) stairway.

7. Their _____ (8 letters) was so clean that one could _____ (5 letters) straight though it.

8. The health and _____ (7 letters) of her constituents _____ (4 letters) of paramount concern to the senator.

9. The _____ (9 letters) was the favorite _____ (4 letters) of transportation of many Presidents.

Answers are on page 80.

10. _____ (6 letters) masks are used by humans at high elevation, but not by _____ (4 letters).

11. The author's _____ (9 letters) showed how a con artist took advantage of a _____ (5 letters) victim.

12. The _____ (10 letters) player was eating a cheeseburger with _____ (5 letters).

13. The _____ (8 letters) and the private were almost bitten by a _____ (5 letters) snake.

14. One often finds an old _____ (6 letters) _____ (4 letters) when digging through the sand in Death Valley.

15. Cardinal and _____ (7 letters) numbers were the topic of her _____ (4 letters) report.

16. The photographer gave _____ (7 letters) on the proper use of a telephoto _____ (4 letters).

17. Commercial success usually requires the _____ (11 letters) of financial backers after you _____ (6 letters) something.

18. President Kennedy gave us the _____ (10 letters) to land a man on the _____ (4 letters).

19. When you wash off a _____ (8 letters) wound, make sure that the water is _____ (4 letters).

20. He _____ (8 letters) learned that he can't _____ (4 letters) on his parents to help him out of trouble.

Answers are on page 80.

Add-On Words

Sometimes, a sentence can be completed sensibly with two words by adding letters to the end of the first missing word to make the second missing word. In these puzzles, the letter counts of both missing words will be provided as a clue. As an example, "I forgot to _____ (5 letters) the _____ (6 letters) door" is sensible with *close* and *closet.*

Find the word pair to solve these puzzles.

1. If you can stand straight against a _____ (4 letters), your _____ (7 letters) will improve.

2. Insiders say it's hard to _____ (5 letters) the _____ (13 letters) business.

3. To get to the barn, you have to walk _____ (4 letters) the _____ (7 letters).

4. Davy Crockett was up _____ (5 letters) about his desire to explore the _____ (8 letters).

5. He did not _____ (3 letters) when he said he filed a _____ (4 letters) against the property.

6. The cowboy with the rusty _____ (4 letters) was _____ (7 letters) by the woman sitting at the bar.

7. Michael Jackson proved that it's not good to _____ (5 letters) a _____ (6 letters).

8. The diner paid _____ (4 letter) for the _____ (6 letters) chicken.

9. The heavyweight _____ (5 letters) celebrated his last victory with _____ (9 letters).

10. I can barely make a _____ (4 letters) in this bill from my _____ (7 letters).

Answers are on page 80.

11. She bought an Asian _____ (4 letters) and some _____ (5 letters) onions.

12. The minister said _____ (4 letters) to the proposed _____ (10 letters) to the church bylaws.

13. My _____ (5 letters) likes to give advice, but it's usually _____ (7 letters).

14. When the weather gets _____ (4 letters), _____ (6 letters) often appears in the basement.

15. Cleaning the chicken _____ (4 letters) will require everybody's _____ (11 letters).

16. The speaker couldn't get people to pay a _____ (4 letters) to hear his talk about the fourth _____ (9 letters).

17. You'd better _____ (5 letters) yourself when you hear about the price of this _____ (8 letters).

18. I can _____ (4 letters) your _____ (5 letters) beating.

19. She bought the _____ (4 letters) in _____ (11 letters) with the brush.

20. Do not allow anyone to _____ (5 letters) your _____ (13 letters) to succeed.

Answers are on page 80.

Part II

SOMETHING IN COMMON

Something in Common Puzzles

Find what all the words in Column A have in common that the words in Column B do not.

Column B words will help you check out your theory for Column A. Here's an example.

COLUMN A	COLUMN B
Glory	Practical
Sword	Yard
Marching	Drum
Coming	Patriotic
Grapes	Sit

Answer: All the words in Column A are in "Battle Hymn of the Republic."

Your solution will be considered correct if it states the right idea in any reasonable way. Please note that Column B is included to eliminate answers that are technically correct, but trivial, such as "words with less than fifteen letters."

Miscellany

Find what all the words in Column A and none of the words in Column B have in common.

1. COLUMN A

Destiny
Quacking
Moderate
Accord
Plaintiff

COLUMN B

Flamingo
Rummage
Innate
Intention
Plaintive

2. COLUMN A

Codicil
Garish
Escarpment
Embassy
Shade

COLUMN B

Council
Indicate
Limerick
Gallon
Predator

3. COLUMN A

Regent
Per
Herd
Clever
Best

COLUMN B

Kept
Model
Scone
Metallic
Pendulum

4. COLUMN A

Train
Mate
Brother
Troubled
Kind

COLUMN B

Fort
Metric
Lemon
Urgent
Calendar

Answers are on page 81.

SOMETHING IN COMMON

Miscellany

5. COLUMN A   COLUMN B

Five	One
Six	Two
Seven	Three
Nine	Four
Ten	Eight

6. COLUMN A   COLUMN B

Swing	Formula
Rider	Master
Bid	Asparagus
Gear	Grow
Note	White

7. COLUMN A   COLUMN B

Snow	Follow
Blood	Park
Note	Yodel
Guard	Crumb
Book	Bonnet

Answers are on page 81.

Miscellany

8. COLUMN A   COLUMN B

Hurt	Pairs
Cast	Resolve
Threes	Quite
Nailed	Left
Manors	Right

9. COLUMN A   COLUMN B

Vanilla	Chocolate
Dry	Beset
Box	Wrestle
Palace	Grain
Nine	Twelve

10. COLUMN A   COLUMN B

Bowling	Marathon
Baseball	Ghost
Union	Rag
Prospecting	Glow
Matches	Circle

Answers are on page 81.

SOMETHING IN COMMON

Miscellany

11. COLUMN A

Cap
Up
No
Cart
Her

COLUMN B

Eat
Down
Yes
Home
May

12. COLUMN A

Chowder
Bisque
Vichyssoise
Borscht
Gazpacho

COLUMN B

Casserole
Meatloaf
Salad
Calzone
Gyro

13. COLUMN A

Marketing
Type
Graph
Vision
Cast

COLUMN B

Council
Indicate
Limerick
Gallon
Predator

14. COLUMN A

Opera
Silica
Flu
Do
Has

COLUMN B

Modern
Camera
Place
Corn
Notch

Answers are on page 81.

15. COLUMN A   COLUMN B

Pebble	Prompt
Palm	Liver
Long	Rate
Cocoa	Order
Myrtle	Placebo

16. COLUMN A   COLUMN B

Potassium	Sodium
King	Queen
Thousand	Hundred
Kosher	Smooth
Constant	Delayed

17. COLUMN A   COLUMN B

Moped	Pride
Bow	Harp
Resume	Mile
Bass	Top
Lead	Flame

18. COLUMN A   COLUMN B

Egg	Prowl
Sweet	Gravel
Basket	Mask
Winner	How
White	Wilt

Answers are on page 81.

SOMETHING IN COMMON

Miscellany

19. COLUMN A   COLUMN B

Question	Koala
Water	Plum
Birth	Furlong
Vaccination	Stand
Bench	Inquest

20. COLUMN A   COLUMN B

Deal	Boat
Valid	Proud
Hint	Time
Valor	Open
Rabble	Rabbit

21. COLUMN A   COLUMN B

Porcine	Cosine
Ovine	Quinine
Bovine	Astatine
Vulpine	Alpine
Lupine	Clandestine

Answers are on page 81.

MENSA SCORING

Average Mensa Score: 30%

Same-Size Words

Find what all the words in Column A and none of the words in Column B have in common.

1. COLUMN A   COLUMN B

Flex	When
Went	Helm
Edit	East
Sage	Hide
Bend	Neck

2. COLUMN A   COLUMN B

Mice	Fade
Door	Dean
Tiny	Sour
Pied	Barn
Lace	Ogle

3. COLUMN A   COLUMN B

Brunt	Baron
Built	Bride
Brand	Bunch
Bloat	Blast
Bloom	Blood

4. COLUMN A   COLUMN B

Pact	Perm
Part	Pout
Pale	Pine
Port	Puck
Pend	Paid

Answers are on page 82.

SOMETHING IN COMMON

Same-Size Words

5. COLUMN A   COLUMN B

COLUMN A	COLUMN B
Limp	Lamp
Fine	Tack
Loud	Male
Dove	Wood
Will	Fire

6. COLUMN A   COLUMN B

COLUMN A	COLUMN B
Metal	Pearl
Canon	Given
Cater	Niche
Boded	Gulch
Taker	Order

7. COLUMN A   COLUMN B

COLUMN A	COLUMN B
Elfin	Cleft
Linen	Laden
Plate	Alive
Bagel	Large
Bleat	Moldy

Answers are on page 82.

Same-Size Words

8. COLUMN A   COLUMN B

COLUMN A	COLUMN B
Slop	Most
Both	Coat
Shot	Port
Stop	Chop
Rots	Poll

9. COLUMN A   COLUMN B

COLUMN A	COLUMN B
Grovel	Corner
Object	Torque
Snored	Operas
Pocket	Sports
Stocks	Column

10. COLUMN A   COLUMN B

COLUMN A	COLUMN B
Many	Carp
Bone	Road
Hero	Lump
Deal	Sold
Room	Each

Answers are on page 82.

SOMETHING IN COMMON

Same-Size Words

11. COLUMN A   COLUMN B

COLUMN A	COLUMN B
Probe	Meter
Crave	Grasp
Frost	Flute
Spike	Break
Bride	Grace

12. COLUMN A   COLUMN B

COLUMN A	COLUMN B
For	Dog
Par	Jar
Pie	Ear
Has	Man
Pat	Hue

13. COLUMN A   COLUMN B

COLUMN A	COLUMN B
Pile	Felt
Slid	Lift
Leer	Last
Lick	Plod
Lest	Lump

14. COLUMN A   COLUMN B

COLUMN A	COLUMN B
Stop	Goes
Rust	Past
Prow	Emit
Upon	Cove
Rosy	Writ

Answers are on page 82.

Same-Size Words

15. COLUMN A   COLUMN B

COLUMN A	COLUMN B
Course	Pardon
Herbal	Harmed
Schism	Detect
Clammy	Sector
Worthy	Bayous

16. COLUMN A   COLUMN B

COLUMN A	COLUMN B
Chic	Full
Plan	Only
Star	Mind
Spun	Hear
Thin	Turn

17. COLUMN A   COLUMN B

COLUMN A	COLUMN B
Douse	Rouse
Amend	Doubt
Orbit	Start
Manor	Green
Heart	Inert

18. COLUMN A   COLUMN B

COLUMN A	COLUMN B
Rite	Race
Oven	Boil
Hole	Held
Ring	Item
Itch	Rope

Answers are on page 82.

SOMETHING IN COMMON

Same-Size Words

19. COLUMN A   COLUMN B

COLUMN A	COLUMN B
Sore	Sips
Sell	Sold
Sort	Such
Suds	Sand
Sire	Soda

20. COLUMN A   COLUMN B

COLUMN A	COLUMN B
Slant	Motor
Climb	Prove
Blare	Sleep
Flour	Orate
Chute	Frill

21. COLUMN A   COLUMN B

COLUMN A	COLUMN B
Coin	Lamb
Rule	Pure
Bale	Vied
Rile	Golf
Cued	Iron

Answers are on page 82.

Answers are on page 82.

MENSA SCORING

Average Mensa Score:	25%

Names & Places

Find what all the words in Column A and none of the words in Column B have in common.

1. COLUMN A   COLUMN B

"You Light Up My Life"	"People Will Say We're In Love"
"True Love"	"I Left My Heart In San Francisco"
"Around the World"	"More"
"Sunrise Sunset"	"I Can't Smile Without You"
"Hello, Young Lovers"	"Love Me Tender"

2. COLUMN A   COLUMN B

It's a Wonderful Life	*Casablanca*
A Hole in the Head	*Harvey*
Arsenic and Old Lace	*Rear Window*
Pocketful of Miracles	*Gone With the Wind*
Mr. Smith Goes to Washington	*To Kill a Mockingbird*

3. COLUMN A   COLUMN B

Punxsutawney	Laredo
Bird-in-Hand	Warm Springs
Valley Forge	Jones Beach
Three-Mile Island	Tulsa
Hershey	Yosemite

Answers are on page 83.

SOMETHING IN COMMON

Names & Places

4. COLUMN A

Guys and Dolls
Hello, Dolly!
West Side Story
On the Town
A Chorus Line

COLUMN B

Flower Drum Song
Carousel
Gigi
Cabaret
La Cage Aux Folles

5. COLUMN A

Oaxaca
Merida
Taxco
Guanajuato
Matamoros

COLUMN B

Santiago
Cuzco
Valladolid
Tegucigalpa
Manila

6. COLUMN A

"Tennessee Waltz"

"Mockingbird Hill"

"Old Cape Cod"

"Changing Partners"

"How Much Is
That Doggie in
the Window?"

COLUMN B

"Any Time"

"Tammy"

"High Hopes"

"Bless Them All"

"Lipstick on Your Collar"

Answers are on page 83.

Names & Places

7. COLUMN A   COLUMN B

The Sun Also Rises	*Hawaii*
For Whom the Bell Tolls	*Exodus*
The Old Man and the Sea	*Catch 22*
A Farewell to Arms	*The Great Gatsby*
To Have and Have Not	*Great Expectations*

8. COLUMN A   COLUMN B

Jeremy Sisto	Sean Connery
James Caviezel	Karl Malden
Jeffrey Hunter	Woody Allen
Robert Powell	Marlon Brando
Ted Neeley	Charlton Heston

9. COLUMN A   COLUMN B

Ansel Adams	Andrew Wyeth
Irving Penn	Hal Holbrook
Dorthea Lange	Ernie Banks
Anne Geddes	Sue Grafton
Stephen Shore	Marie Curie

Answers are on page 83.

SOMETHING IN COMMON

Names & Places

10. COLUMN A COLUMN B

Enquirer *Herald Tribune*
Plain Dealer *Republic*
Dispatch *Star News*
Beacon Journal *News Examiner*
Blade *Free Press*

11. COLUMN A COLUMN B

Cornell Harvard
Rensselaer Rutgers
Polytechnic
Columbia Stanford
Barnard Brigham Young
Vassar Brown

12. COLUMN A COLUMN B

Tupelo Salt Lake City
Corinth Buffalo
Philadelphia Des Moines
Oxford Tulsa
Biloxi Bangor

Answers are on page 83.

Names & Places

13. COLUMN A

"Once in Love
with Amy"

"Luck Be a Lady"

"If I Were a Bell"

"Standing on
the Corner"

"I Believe in You"

COLUMN B

"A Wonderful Guy"

"Hey There"

"On the Street
Where You Live"

"Old Man River"

"Maria"

14. COLUMN A

France
Portugal
Argentina
Australia
Haiti

COLUMN B

Germany
Brazil
Poland
Norway
Russia

15. COLUMN A

Montreal
New York
Atlanta
Bogata
Havana

COLUMN B

Denver
Tokyo
Chicago
Paris
Jerusalem

Answers are on page 83.

SOMETHING IN COMMON

Names & Places

16. COLUMN A

Saint Paul
Memphis
Saint Louis
Baton Rouge
Moline

COLUMN B

Indianapolis
Des Moines
Kansas City
Albuquerque
Omaha

17. COLUMN A

Celine Dion
Paul Anka
Anne Murray
K. D. Lang
Alanis Morissette

COLUMN B

Frank Sinatra
Eminem
Marvin Gaye
Eddie Fisher
Luciano Pavarotti

18. COLUMN A

Maine
New York
California
Texas
North Dakota

COLUMN B

Virginia
West Virginia
Oregon
Florida
Arkansas

Answers are on page 83.

Names & Places

19. COLUMN A   COLUMN B

Las Vegas	Omaha
Portland	Miami
Denver	Indianapolis
New York	Reno
Detroit	San Diego

20. COLUMN A   COLUMN B

The Terminator	*Rocky*
Bedtime for Bonzo	*The Sting*
Running Man	*Casablanca*
Kindergarten Cop	*Pretty Woman*
Predator	*Get Shorty*

21. COLUMN A   COLUMN B

Joe Montana	Doug Flutie
Paul Hornung	Randall Cunningham
Joe Theisman	Warren Moon
John Huarte	Dan Marino
Terry Hanratty	Joe Namath

Answers are on page 83.

SOMETHING IN COMMON

MENSA SCORING

| Average Mensa Score: | 30% |

Name Shuffles

KID-FRIENDLY BONUS

These sentences can all be completed and make sense with a name and its anagram (rearranging the letters). Here's an example:

_____ wanted to _____ another piece of candy.

Answer: Kate and take

Find the name and its anagram.

1. _____ keeps up with current _____ by reading the newspaper.

2. _____ saw a weather _____ on a farm building.

3. _____ wanted to explore a _____ reef.

4. _____ forgot to turn on the _____ conditioner.

5. _____ thinks his ill-mannered little sister is a real _____.

6. _____ bought three lemons and two _____.

7. _____ likes to _____ his head in agreement.

8. _____ was concerned that her dog had too much _____ on its skin.

9. _____ couldn't go because his cold _____ up.

10. _____ tried out for track _____ field.

Answers are on page 83.

MENSA SCORING

Average Mensa Score:	75%

Part III

SPECIAL DAYS

Valentine's Day

Fill in the blanks with the missing letters to form a word, name, or phrase associated with Valentine's Day. Please note that Hangman rules don't apply, and sometimes the same letter may be exposed someplace and hidden in other places. Here's an example: __ O D __ __ A __ H __ C O __ __ T E __

Answer: Godiva chocolates.

Find lovely solutions to these puzzles.

1. __ H __ T M __ __ ' __ __ A __ P L __ __

2. __ Y __ U __ __ Y __ A __ E __ __ __ __ E

3. __ W __ E __ __ O __ H __ N __ __

4. B A __ __ Y __ A __ I L __ __ S O __ __ S

5. O __ __ T E __ S __ N __ __ H A __ P A __ __ __

6. __ O __ A __ C __

7. B __ __ __ __ Z __ F __ __ H __ __ __ M __ R __

8. __ E __ R U __ R __ __ O __ __ T __ E __ T __

9. __ V __ __ P __ I __ E __ __ E __ T __ U __ A __ __

10. A __ __ R O __ I T __

Answers are on page 84.

St. Patrick's Day

Fill in the blanks with the missing letters to form a word, name, or phrase associated with St. Patrick's Day. Please note that Hangman rules don't apply, and sometimes the same letter may be exposed someplace and hidden in other places. Here's an example: _ M E _ _ _ D   I _ _ _

Answer: Emerald Isle

Find lucky solutions to these puzzles.

1. _ U _ N N _ _ S

2. P _ _ _ _ Y   _ _ O _ S

3. _ O _ D _ N _ E _ _ Y   A _ _

4. K _ _ _ E _   T _ _   _ N _ K _ _

5. H A _ _ I _ A _

6. _ _ B E _ N _ A _

7. _ O U _ _ Y   _ O _ K

8. H _ R _   _ U S _ _

9. _ A M _ _   J _ _ C _

10. A _ D _   C A _ _

Answers are on page 84.

MENSA SCORING

Average Mensa Score:	35%

Independence Day

Fill in the blanks with the missing letters to form a word, name, or phrase associated with Independence Day. Please note that Hangman rules don't apply, and sometimes the same letter may be exposed someplace and hidden in other places. Here's an example: P __ __ L __ __ E __ __ H __ __

Answer: Philadelphia

Find solutions to these puzzles independently.

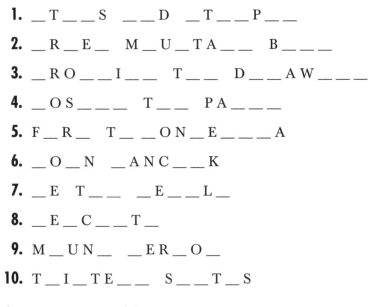

1. __ T __ __ S __ __ D __ T __ __ P __ __

2. __ R E __ M __ U __ T A __ __ B __ __ __

3. __ R O __ __ I __ __ T __ __ D __ __ A W __ __ __

4. __ O S __ __ __ T __ __ P A __ __ __

5. F __ R __ T __ __ O N __ E __ __ __ A

6. __ O __ N __ A N C __ __ K

7. __ E T __ __ __ E __ __ L __

8. __ E __ C __ __ T __

9. M __ U N __ __ E R __ O __

10. T __ I __ T E __ __ S __ __ T __ S

Answers are on page 84.

Labor Day

Fill in the blanks with the missing letters to form a word, name, or phrase associated with Labor Day. Please note that Hangman rules don't apply, and sometimes the same letter may be exposed someplace and hidden in other places. Here's an example: _ I _ K E _   L _ _ E

Answer: picket line

Find solutions to these puzzles with a minimum of labor.

1. _ E _ E F _ _ S

2. S _ _ I A _   _ E _ U R _ _ _ _

3. _ N _ O _   _ U E _

4. P _ I _   _ A _ A _ I _ _ _

5. O _ _ R _ I _ _

6. _ _ Y C _ _ _ _

7. _ O _ K   _ T O _ _ A _ _

8. _ R _ I T _ _ T _ _ _

9. S _ _ I _ _   F _ _ D

10. U _ _ T _ _   A _ T _   _ O _ K _ _ S

Answers are on page 85.

MENSA SCORING

Average Mensa Score:	55%

Columbus Day

Fill in the blanks with the missing letters to form a word, name, or phrase associated with Columbus Day. Please note that Hangman rules don't apply, and sometimes the same letter may be exposed someplace and hidden in other places. Here's an example: __ __ W __ O __ L D

Answer: New World

Discover solutions to these puzzles.

1. E __ __ L O __ __ R
2. __ __ __ G __ E __ D I __ __ N __
3. __ E __ __ A
4. L O __ __ I __ __ __ O __ I __ D __ __
5. __ __ N D __ __ O __ __ I __ P __ __ O __ __
6. N __ __ __
7. __E __ E L __ Y
8. __ R __ U __ H __ D __ __ E __ S __
9. C __ O __ __ E __ A __ L __ N __ I __
10. __ C __ O __ E __ T __ __ L __ T __

Answers are on page 85.

Mensa Scoring

Average Mensa Score: 40%

Part IV

CELEBRITIES

Singers

The sentence, "The shirt that I _____ be usable as a rag," can be completed with the sound of TORME (tore may).

Find a famous singer's last name that sounds like familiar words to complete these sentences so that they make sense.

1. If you took a picture of Big _____ means you have been to London.

2. Was the Wizard of _____ in the month of January?

3. She put advancement in her _____ her number one goal.

4. Whenever she eats _____ skin breaks out in a rash.

5. Should the sign of the _____ made when you enter this church?

6. Lifting weights will make your _____.

7. The eccentric person who wanted a metal toilet just had a _____ installed.

8. A new house in this area will _____ T-S of money.

9. When your supply of Lifesavers is running _____ may be a good substitute.

10. _____ get defeated by Grant because he underestimated his abilities?

Answers are on page 86.

Singers

11. For some people, the best destination in _____ Nice.

12. Whether on sea _____ comes right before *p*.

13. There are four _____ a deck of cards.

14. The accountant tried to explain _____ profits dropped even though sales increased.

15. Does the archer lifting the _____ how to shoot an arrow?

16. The aquarium has eight shark tanks, nine stingray tanks, and _____ tanks.

17. Some people scream and _____ after day.

18. _____ the telephone booth changing into Superman.

19. They used _____ many cat food commercials.

20. After the introduction of the Big _____ carloads of people went to the golden arches.

Answers are on page 86.

Mensa Scoring

Average Mensa Score:	50%

CELEBRITIES

Actors

The sentence, "Automatic transmissions use a _____ the symbol for high, forward gear," can be completed with the sound of DIAZ (*D* as).

Find a well-known actor or actress's last name that sounds like familiar words to complete these sentences so that they make sense.

1. _____ of dandruff fell on his shirt collar.

2. In the coin shop, the father told his little boy, "That's a buffalo _____."

3. Did Ernie ever _____ home on Sesame Street?

4. Did the makers of Canada _____ over the formula for their ginger ale?

5. _____ visors on the passenger's side often have mirrors.

6. A person who strictly observes Passover must _____ from being baked into any foods.

7. Did the student who deserved a _____ the professor into giving him a higher grade?

8. Does the swap meet merchant in that _____ its products or sell them on consignment?

9. The majority of voters did not like _____ than Lyndon in 1964.

10. The prospective buyer carefully _____ and Chrysler sales literature.

Answers are on page 86.

11. He claims he was raised in a tiny _____ the middle of the jungle.

12. If the room is decorated in _____ means they're expecting a girl.

13. They _____ than one hundred feet down before they struck oil.

14. Traveling _____ be easier on motorists at twilight compared with going the other way.

15. Some people seem to be a little too _____ little too long when meeting strangers.

16. Mrs. Rather was worried that she and _____ would be late for school.

17. A good doorbell usually has a _____.

18. Mr. Jones retired, but a _____ was hired to take his place.

19. The man who saw the "NO LOGGING" _____ the tree anyway.

20. When you get _____ me at the office.

Answers are on page 86.

CELEBRITIES

Athletes

The sentence, "I left the inventory _____ my briefcase," can be completed with the sound of LISTON (list in).

Find a famous athlete's last name that sounds like familiar words to complete these sentences so that they make sense.

1. She ended her shopping _____ past six o'clock.

2. When a seamstress _____ button, it must be the right size.

3. The _____ be on sale near Easter and Christmas.

4. Did reporters ever _____ Fitzgerald's yard?

5. The nouveau _____ moving into more and more old-money neighborhoods.

6. Does a typical _____ as much military history as a naval officer?

7. The bakery has three dozen loaves of _____ the display case.

8. Do many people who buy an antique _____ the purchase because of the upkeep expense?

9. He will either make _____ have to stay in jail.

10. The coffee drinker took a _____ few dollars, then left.

Answers are on page 87.

11. Does your razor _____ often than mine?

12. She once _____ Norris practicing Kung Fu moves.

13. Eating too much can change a small guy into a _____.

14. When you meet a strange dog, you should _____ under the chin.

15. Let the _____ kneaded thoroughly.

16. _____ after Mark and before John.

17. Bad hops will _____.

18. If you're hit by a hockey _____ will hurt.

19. Some people love to eat a _____ chocolate sundae.

20. Are there many movies that _____ St. John?

Answers are on page 87.

CELEBRITIES

Sam, Dan & Ron Are Hiding

KID-FRIENDLY BONUS

Sometimes names can be hiding inside some consecutive letters of words. For example, the name *Ron* can be hiding in a word that means the beginning of a line: F*RON*T. Below you'll find hints for common words that contain the names Sam, Dan, or Ron.

Find Sam, Dan, or Ron hiding in the following words.

1. The opposite of safety

2. A type of seed

3. A large dinosaur

4. Small taste

5. A colorful weed

6. Right away

7. From Denmark

8. The largest city in Canada

9. Identical

10. The royal seat

Answers are on page 87.

Mensa Scoring

Average Mensa Score: 80%

Part V

HIDDEN THINGS

Hidden Math Words

A word relating to mathematics or geometry can be hiding in the consecutive letters within a sentence. For example, "They knew that they had done the wrong thing" is hiding the word *ADD* in "hAD Done" found in the middle of the sentence.

Find the math or geometry word that is hiding in the consecutive letters within these sentences.

1. They watched the Raiders outplay the Broncos in every aspect of the game.

2. He gave his pet serpent a gondola ride.

3. How did the koala cub end up with the kangaroos?

4. Did the kind entomologist pamper centipedes?

5. Many people find it hard to sing "The Star Spangled Banner."

6. The scholarship includes tuition but does not cover textbooks.

7. The governor gave the budget a cut everywhere possible.

8. It is rumored that Capri men often marry Naples women.

9. He drove his new Mustang entirely too recklessly.

10. Groucho and Harpo were two of the Marx brothers.

Answers are on page 88.

Answers are on page 88.

Mensa Scoring	
Average Mensa Score:	95%

Hidden Automobile Models

An automobile model can be hiding in the consecutive letters within a sentence. For example, "A defector from Epsilon Delta Tau rushed a different fraternity" is hiding the brand name TAURUS in the words "TAU RUShed." Find the automobile model that is hiding in the consecutive letters within these sentences.

1. The zookeeper gave the chimp a large banana.

2. The police had the home of the pyromaniac cordoned off.

3. This recipe calls for only one onion.

4. In order to accommodate another animal I built a new cage.

5. The actress made a first-class entrance.

6. Did Indiana ever finish fourth under Bird?

7. There are galactic areas where our starship has not traveled.

8. Without a whimper I altered the will, as suggested by my attorney.

9. Do math majors find people with a nice compass attractive?

10. I once saw a gambler from Mexico roll a seven five times in a row.

Answers are on page 88.

Hidden Authors

The last name of a famous author can be hiding in consecutive letters within a sentence. For example, "I didn't enjoy certain things about that movie" is hiding the author JOYCE, found in "enJOY CErtain" in the middle of the sentence. Find the author who is hiding in the consecutive letters within these sentences.

1. Using a detour is the only way to get there.

2. In the story of corrupt leaders, the saga never ends.

3. I wish utensils were less expensive at this store.

4. A typical graduate of Vassar treasures her alma mater.

5. I was told that a zircon radiates as much light as a diamond.

6. I call my mother's smart sibling Uncle Mensa.

7. The total cotton crop profit was just under fifty thousand dollars.

8. The prototype of a racer van tested out rather well.

9. Who is that thug over there?

10. The veggie burger tasted just like real beef.

Answers are on page 89.

Part VI

SYNANAGRAMS

States & Provinces in North America

First find the synonym for the word suggested by crossword-style clues; the number of letters for the word is in parentheses. Then rearrange the letters of each synonym to find the place name of a state or province in North America.

For example, if the word clues are "also (3) + precipitation (4)," the synonyms would be TOO and RAIN, which can be rearranged into the place name ONTARIO.

Combine your synonym and anagram skills to find these states and provinces in the United States, Canada, and Mexico.

1. Knight's mail (5) + fighter jet (3)

2. Fish eggs (3) + holiday drink (3)

3. Like (2) + career (8)

4. Fuss (3) + hello (2)

5. Portal (4) + form of carbon (4)

6. Rowing tool (3) + male offspring (3)

7. Combine (3) + bovine (3) + originally surnamed (3)

8. Primary (4) + vessel (4)

9. Achieves victory (4) + metal money (5)

10. Awestruck (4) + anger (3)

Answers are on page 90.

Mensa Scoring	
Average Mensa Score:	50%

Chemical Elements

First find the synonym for the word suggested by crossword-style clues; the number of letters for the word is in parentheses. Then rearrange the letters of each synonym to find the name of a chemical element.

For example, for the word clues "prohibit (3) + mythical bird (3)," the synonyms are BAN and ROC, which can be rearranged into CARBON.

Combine your synonym and anagram skills to find these other elements.

1. Wedding symbol (4) + get muscular (4)

2. Twelfth of a foot (4) + folktales (4)

3. Automobile (3) + opposite over hypotenuse (4)

4. Exterminator's house covering (4) + firearms (4)

5. Spicy Indian food (5) + solver of this puzzle (2)

6. Sing without words (3) + portions of bytes (4)

7. Graduates (6) + Greek *m* (2)

8. Scott Joplin composition (3) + negative (2)

9. Leave out (4) + changes directions (5)

10. Minuscule (4) + groan's companion (4)

Answers are on page 90.

SYNANANAGRAMS

Mensa Scoring

Average Mensa Score:	50%

Professional Sports Teams

First find the synonym for the word suggested by crossword-style clues; the number of letters for the word is in parentheses. Then rearrange the letters of each synonym to find the name of a professional sports team.

For example, if the word clues are "door opener (3) + mentally sound (4)," the synonyms would be KEY and SANE, which can be rearranged into YANKEES.

Combine your synonym and anagram skills to find professional sports teams.

1. For each (3) + wine barrel (4)

2. Watermelon covering (4) + sea lion cousins (5)

3. Canine (3) + Communists (4)

4. Face cover (4) + performed (3) + BLT meat (5)

5. Can metal (3) + droop (3)

6. Rio's country (6) + less fresh (6)

7. Got up (4) + Exxon's business (3)

8. Words of action (5) + indefinite article (1)

9. Canine itch cause (5) + sufficient (5)

10. Obtain (3) + knight's title (3)

Answers are on page 91.

Mensa Scoring	
Average Mensa Score:	45%

National Parks

First find the synonym for the word suggested by crossword-style clues; the number of letters for the word is in parentheses. Then rearrange the letters of each synonym to find the name of a national park in the United States.

For example, if the word clues are "portal (4) + married (3)," the synonyms are DOOR and WED, which can be rearranged into REDWOOD.

Combine your synonym and anagram skills to find these other national parks.

1. Leave out (4) + sight organs (4)

2. Mom's mother (6) + is capable of (3) + perform (2)

3. Unique (3) + water storage devices (5) + plaything (3)

4. Crushed rocks (6) + watermelon pit (4)

5. Female turkey (3) + possesses (3) + commercial message (2) + not off (2)

6. Risotto ingredient (4) + be behind (3)

7. Wrote down (5) + Say yes to a request for money (5)

8. Hunter (7) + beer's cousin (3)

9. Strongly desire (5) + lacking any tang (5) + ugly marks (5)

10. Place where one lies (3) + Crosby's first name (4)

Answers are on page 91.

Answers are on page 91.

SYNANANAGRAMS

Mensa Scoring

Average Mensa Score:	30%

Dog & Cat Breeds

First find the synonym for the word suggested by crossword-style clues; the number of letters for the word is in parentheses. Then rearrange the letters of each synonym to find the name of a dog or cat breed.

For example, if the word clues are "close to (4) + drink slowly (3)," the synonyms are NEAR and SIP, which can be rearranged into PERSIAN.

Combine your synonym and anagram skills to find these other dog and cat breeds.

1. Pea covering (3) + astrological lion (3)

2. Sweet potato (3) + unit of medication (4)

3. Castrated horse (7) + has aspirations (5) + that female (3)

4. Goal (3) + perceives (4)

5. Not smooth (5) + turn down (4)

6. Goof (4) + item for a camera (4) + didn't play (3)

7. Batters (7) + father (4)

8. Male goose (6) + consume (3)

9. Unrestricted choice (3) + unwarranted preference (4) + trespass (3)

10. Brief sleep (3) + Caesar salad lettuce (7)

Answers are on page 92.

Answers are on page 92.

Mensa Scoring

Average Mensa Score:	30%

Incomplete Alphabet Messages

BONUS

Certain common expressions can be formed by writing an alphabet with some letters removed.

For example, ABCDEFHIJKMPQRSTUVWXYZ can be interpreted as "LONG absence" since the letters in LONG are absent. (The letters G L N O are rearranged for the word LONG.)

Use the incomplete alphabets below to find the expressions. The word formed from the missing letters comes first in the common expression.

1. ABCEFHIJKLMNPQRSTUVWXYZ

2. BDEFHJKLMOPQRSUVWXYZ

3. BCFGHIJKMNOPQSTUVWXZ

4. ABDFGHJKLMNOPQRSUVXYZ

5. ABCEFGHIJKLMPQRTVWXYZ

6. ABCDEFGHIJKLMOPQSTVWXYZ

7. ACFGHIJKMNPQRSTVWXYZ

8. ABCDEFHJKMPQRTUVXYZ

9. ABCDEFGHIJKLMOPQSVWXYZ

10. BEFGHJKMNOPQRSUVXYZ

Answers are on page 92.

SYNANANAGRAMS

Mensa Scoring	
Average Mensa Score:	55%

ANSWERS

Part I
Quick Word Puzzles

ANSWERS

Q Puzzles 1

1. Torquemada and Inquisition
2. Quatre and cinq
3. squadron and Iraqi
4. pique and misquoted
5. coquettish and mystique
6. acquittal and Marquis
7. quahog and bisque
8. mosquito and quinine
9. croque and quiche
10. quadratic and square

Puzzles on page 8

J Puzzles 3

1. majority and Jordan
2. Judo and dojo
3. jereboam and rioja
4. reject and Juarez
5. Pajama and Jackson
6. banjo and adjust
7. jojoba and jarring (or jumping)
8. Dijon and marjoram
9. Judge and Judy
10. jetsam and fjord

Puzzles on page 10

Z Puzzles 2

1. Zinc and oxidize
2. Belize and Brazil
3. ouzo and bouzouki
4. Lizzy and Dizzy
5. Mozart and Salzburg
6. ozone and hazy
7. Bonzo and zoo
8. czar and zealot
9. Zinfandel and appetizer
10. Wizard and Liza

Puzzles on page 9

X Puzzles 4

1. pixels and exponentially
2. crux and sexist
3. executive and proxy
4. Botox and toxic
5. matrix and Excel
6. extraordinary and coxswain
7. express and Bronx
8. Oaxaca and Mexico
9. latex and peroxide
10. luxury and tax

Puzzles on page 11

K Puzzles

1. knack and kowtowing
2. skein and nickel
3. Klondike and breakneck
4. Lakers and Knicks
5. knife and backpack
6. strikes and turkey
7. Kennedy and Kerry
8. knockwurst (or knackwurst) and sauerkraut
9. Kennebunkport and blanketed (or blockaded)
10. bookkeeper and acknowledged

Puzzles on page 12

Movies—the 1980s

1. *Silverado*
2. *Atlantic City*
3. *Dirty Rotten Scoundrels*
4. *American Gigolo*
5. *Scarface*
6. *Neighbors*
7. *Weird Science*
8. *Broadway Danny Rose*
9. *Gorky Park*
10. *Trading Places*

11. *Private Benjamin*
12. *Lethal Weapon*
13. *Caddyshack*
14. *Ordinary People*
15. *Hairspray*
16. *The Verdict*
17. *Jagged Edge*
18. *The Fourth Protocol*
19. *Risky Business*
20. *Extreme Prejudice*

Puzzles on page 13

Puzzles on page 14

Non-Repeaters

1. resumption
2. abolishment
3. personality
4. formulating
5. speculation
6. obfuscating
7. conjugated
8. journalism
9. normalized
10. percolating

Puzzles on page 15

11. subordinate
12. chlorinated
13. problematic
14. ambidextrous
15. background
16. misfortune
17. sympathize
18. Smoldering
    (or squelching)
19. copyrightable
20. authorized

Puzzles on page 16

Holiday Season Letter Zappers

1. wreath
2. nativity
3. "Silent Night"
4. mistletoe
5. holy infant
6. "Over the River"
7. yuletide
8. Bethlehem
9. Kwanzaa
10. "Little Drummer Boy"

Puzzles on page 17

11. Prince of Peace
12. Three wise men
13. "Frosty the Snowman"
14. Saint Nicholas
15. pumpkin pie
16. *Feliz Navidad*
17. Hanukah (alternate
    spelling of Chanukah)
18. "Auld Lang Syne"
19. seasons greetings
    (or seasons' greetings)
20. Santa Claus

Puzzles on page 18

1. Warren Harding
2. Franklin Pierce
3. Martin Van Burin
4. Ulysses Grant
5. John Kennedy
6. William Clinton
7. William Taft
8. Ronald Reagan
9. Herbert Hoover
10. Dwight Eisenhower

11. George Bush
12. Franklin Roosevelt
13. James Madison
14. Gerald Ford
15. Theodore Roosevelt
16. James Carter
17. Lyndon Johnson
18. George Washington
19. Richard Nixon
20. Grover Cleveland

Puzzles on page 19

Puzzles on page 20

1. ET/ETA (or ETD)
2. CP/CPA
3. TV/TVA
4. JD/JDL
5. MP/MPG
6. LC/LCM or LCD
   (least common multiple
   or denominator)
7. FD/FDA
8. AA/AAA
9. MS/MSG
10. PD/PDA

11. AM/AMC
12. AL/ALS
13. BS/BSA
14. PC/PCH
15. PT/PTA
16. PG/PGA
17. DA/DAR
18. CB/CBS
19. PH/PHD
20. DD/DDT

Puzzles on page 22

Puzzles on page 21

Drop Letters

1. platinum and plum
   (or haggard and hard)
2. radiation and radon
3. accusation and action
4. hateful and haul
   (or toyless and toss)
5. amounting and among
6. spiritual and spiral
7. stemware and stare
8. welfare and were
9. motorcade and mode
   (or limousine and line)

Puzzles on page 23

10. Oxygen and oxen
11. narrative and naïve
12. backgammon and bacon
13. corporal and coral
14. bovine and bone
15. ordinal and oral
16. lessons and lens
17. involvement and invent
18. motivation and moon
19. puncture and pure
20. recently and rely

Puzzles on page 24

Add-On Words

1. post and posture
2. enter and entertainment
3. past and pasture
4. front and frontier
5. lie and lien
6. spur and spurned
7. singe and singer
8. cash and cashew
9. champ and champagne
10. dent and dentist

Puzzles on page 25

11. pear and pearl
12. amen and amendments
13. uncle and unclear
14. mild and mildew
15. coop and cooperation
16. dime and dimension
17. brace and bracelet
18. hear and heart
19. comb and combination
20. deter and determination

Puzzles on page 26

Part II
Something in Common

ANSWERS

Miscellany

1. All end in four letters that form a word.
2. All have a fish buried within the word (cod, gar, etc.).
3. All can form a new word by putting *a* after first *e*.
4. All can form an expression with *soul*.
5. All letters are made from straight lines only.
6. All can form an expression with *low* (or *high*).
7. All can form an expression with *bank*.
8. All can anagram into a book of the Bible (Ruth, Acts, etc.).
9. All can form an expression with *ice*.
10. All can be associated with *strike* or *strikes*.
11. All can form a new word when followed by *on*.
12. All are soups.
13. All can from a new word when preceded with *tele*.
14. All can form a new word when followed by *te*.
15. All are names of well-known beaches.
16. All may be symbolized with *k* or *K*.
17. All can be pronounced more than one way.
18. All can form an expression or word with *bread*.
19. All can form an expression with *mark*.
20. All can form a new word by replacing the first letter with *squ*.
21. All pertain to animals.

Puzzles on pages 29–34

2

1. All can form a new word if *e* is changed to *a*.
2. All can form a new word if *n* is added after the second letter.
3. All can form a new word if *b* is changed to *g*.
4. All can form a new word when preceded with *im*.
5. All can form a new word by replacing the first letter with *shr*.
6. All can form a new word if *n* is added after the second letter; a dejá-vu of puzzle 2.
7. All can form a new word by eliminating *e* and *l*.
8. All can form a new word by replacing *o* with *oo*.
9. All can form a new word by changing *o* to *a*.
10. All can form a new word by changing the first letter to *z*.
11. All can form a new word by changing the fourth letter to *n*.
12. All can form a new word when followed by *ty*.
13. All can form a new word by replacing *l* with *qu*.
14. All words use only the second half of the alphabet (n–z).
15. All words have a possessive pronoun buried in it (our, her, etc.).
16. All can form a new word when followed by *k*.
17. All consist of a 2-letter word followed by a 3-letter word.
18. All can form a new word when preceded with *w*.
19. All can form a new word by inserting *p* after the first letter.
20. All can form a new word by changing the last two letters to *ck*.
21. All can form a new word by inserting *ff* after the second letter.

Puzzles on pages 35–40

1. All are in $\frac{3}{4}$ (waltz) tempo.
2. All are directed by Frank Capra.
3. All are in Pennsylvania.
4. All are set in New York City.
5. All are in Mexico.
6. All were sung by Patty Paige.
7. All were written by Ernest Hemingway.
8. All had a starring role playing Jesus.
9. All were famous photographers.
10. All are Ohio city newspapers.
11. All are in New York state.
12. All are in Mississippi.
13. All are written by Frank Loesser.
14. All are spelled the same way in the country's native language.
15. All are in the eastern standard time zone.
16. All border the Mississippi River.
17. All were born in Canada.
18. All have a land border with a neighboring country.
19. All have more consonants than vowels.
20. All feature an actor-turned-governor (Schwarzenegger, Reagan, Ventura).
21. All played quarterback for Notre Dame.

Puzzles on pages 41–47

Name Shuffles (Kid-Friendly Bonus) ⬛4

1. Steven and events
2. Evan and vane
3. Carol (or Carlo) and coral
4. Ira (or Ari) and air
5. Bart and brat
6. Miles and limes
7. Don and nod
8. Megan and mange
9. Alfred and flared
10. Dan and and

Puzzles on page 48

Part III
Special Days

ANSWERS

Valentine's Day **1**

1. Whitman's Sampler
2. "My Funny Valentine"
3. Sweet nothings
4. Barry Manilow songs
5. Oysters and champagne
6. Romance
7. Bonanza for Hallmark
8. February fourteenth
9. Overpriced restaurant
10. Aphrodite

Puzzles on page 50

St. Patrick's Day **2**

1. Guinness
2. Pointy shoes
3. Londonderry Air
4. Killed the snakes
5. Harrigan
6. Hibernian
7. County Cork
8. Harp music
9. James Joyce
10. Andy Capp

Puzzles on page 51

Independence Day **3**

1. Stars and Stripes
2. Green Mountain Boys
3. Crossing the Delaware
4. Boston Tea Party
5. Fort Ticonderoga
6. John Hancock
7. We the People
8. Redcoats
9. Mount Vernon
10. Thirteen states

Puzzles on page 52

Labor Day   **4**

1. Benefits
2. Social security
3. Union dues
4. Paid vacations
5. Overtime
6. Boycott
7. Work stoppage
8. Arbitration
9. Strike fund
10. United Auto Workers

Puzzles on page 53

Columbus Day   **5**

1. Explorer
2. King Ferdinand
3. Genoa
4. Looking for India
5. Landed on Hispanola
6. Nina
7. Jewelry
8. Brought disease
9. Crossed Atlantic
10. October Twelfth

Puzzles on page 54

SPECIAL DAYS

Part IV
Celebrities

ANSWERS

Singers

1

1. Bennett (Ben, it)
2. Osbourne (Oz born)
3. Carreras (career as)
4. Fisher (fish her)
5. Crosby (cross be)
6. Armstrong (arm strong)
7. Newton-John (new tin john)
8. Costello (cost L-O-)
9. Lopez (low, Pez)
10. Diddley (Did Lee)

Puzzles on page 56

11. Francis (France is)
12. Orlando (or land, *o*)
13. Jackson (jacks in)
14. Wynette (why net)
15. Bono (bow know)
16. Tennille (ten eel)
17. Holiday (holler day)
18. Clarkson (Clark's in)
19. Morrison (Morris in)
20. McEntire (Mac, entire)

Puzzles on page 57

Actors

2

1. Affleck (a fleck)
2. Nicholson (nickel, son)
3. Roberts (rob Bert's)
4. Dreyfuss (Dry fuss)
5. Carson (Car sun)
6. Bardot (bar dough)
7. Deitrich (*D* trick)
8. Stallone (stall own)
9. Barrymore (Barry more)
10. Redford (read Ford)

Puzzles on page 58

11. Hutton (hut in)
12. Pinckett (pink it)
13. Douglas (dug less)
14. Eastwood (east would)
15. Fonda (fond a)
16. Danson (Dan's son)
17. Gooding (good ding)
18. Newman (new man)
19. Seinfeld (sign felled)
20. Bacall (back, call)

Puzzles on page 59

Athletes

1. Sprewell (spree well)
2. Sosa (sews a)
3. Hamill (ham'll)
4. Campanella (camp in Ella)
5. Richard (riche are)
6. Marino (marine know)
7. Ryan (rye in)
8. Carew (car rue)
9. Baylor (bail or)
10. Cepeda (sip, paid a)

Puzzles on page 60

11. Nicklaus (nick less)
12. Sawchuk (saw Chuck)
13. Largent (large gent)
14. Pettit or Pettitte (pet it)
15. Doby (dough be)
16. Lucas (Luke is)
17. Killebrew (kill a brew)
18. Puckett (puck it)
19. Goodrich (good rich)
20. Stargell (star Jill)– also Starr (star)

Puzzles on page 61

Sam, Dan & Ron Are Hiding (Kid-Friendly Bonus)

1. danger (DANger)
2. sesame (seSAMe)
3. brontosaurus (bRONtosaurus)
4. sample (SAMple)
5. dandelion (DANdelion)
6. pronto (pRONto)
7. Danish (DANish)–also Dane (DANe)
8. Toronto (ToRONto)
9. same (SAMe)
10. throne (thRONe)

Puzzles on page 62

Part V
Hidden Things

ANSWERS

Hidden Math Words ▮**1**

1. cosine (BronCOS IN Every)
2. pentagon (serPENT A GONdola)
3. cube (CUB End)
4. percent (pamPER CENTipedes)
5. angle (SpANGLEd)
6. vertex (coVER TEXt)
7. acute (A CUT Everywhere)
8. prime (CaPRI MEn)
9. tangent (MusTANG ENTirely)
10. power (HarPO WERe)

Puzzles on page 64

Hidden Automobile Models ▮**2**

1. Impala (chIMP A LArge)
2. Accord (pyromaniAC CORDoned)
3. Neon (oNE ONion)
4. Malibu (aniMAL I BUilt)
5. Sentra (clasS ENTRAnce)
6. Thunderbird (fourTH UNDER BIRD)
7. Regal (aRE GALaxies)
8. Imperial (wIMPER I ALtered)
9. Passat (comPASS ATtractive)
10. Corolla (MexiCO ROLL A)

Puzzles on page 65

3

1. Uris (detoUR IS)
2. Sagan (SAGA Never)
3. Shute (wiSH UTEnsils)
4. Sartre (VasSAR TREasures)
5. Conrad (zirCON RADiates)
6. Clemens (UnCLE MENSa)
7. Alcott (totAL COTTon)
8. Cervantes (raCER VAN TESted)
9. Hugo (tHUG Over)
10. Albee (reAL BEEf)

Puzzles on page 66

Puzzles on page 66

HIDDEN THINGS

Part VI
Synanagrams

ANSWERS

States & Provinces in North America 1

1. Michigan (chain + Mig)
2. Oregon (roe + nog)
3. Nova Scotia (as + vocation)
4. Idaho (ado + hi)
5. Colorado (door + coal)
6. Sonora (oar + son)
7. New Mexico (mix + cow + nee)
8. Manitoba (main + boat)
9. Wisconsin (wins + coins)
10. Georgia (agog + ire)

Puzzles on page 68

Puzzles on page 68

Chemical Elements 2

1. Nitrogen (ring + tone)
2. Chlorine (inch + lore)
3. Arsenic (car + sine)
4. Tungsten (tent + guns)
5. Mercury (curry + me)
6. Bismuth (hum + bits)
7. Aluminum (alumni + mu)
8. Argon (rag + no)
9. Strontium (omit + turns)
10. Antimony (tiny + moan)

Puzzles on page 69

Puzzles on page 69

Professional Sports Teams

1. Packers (per + cask)
2. Islanders (rind + seals)
3. Dodgers (dog + Reds)
4. Diamondbacks (mask + did + bacon)
5. Giants (tin + sa g)
6. Trailblazers (Brazil + staler)
7. Orioles (rose + oil)
8. Braves (verbs + a)
9. Maple Leafs (fleas + ample)
10. Tigers (get + sir)

Puzzles on page 70

National Parks

1. Yosemite (omit + eyes)
2. Grand Canyon (granny + can + do)
3. Yellowstone (one + wells + toy)
4. Everglades (gravel + seed)
5. Shenandoah (hen + has + ad + on)
6. Glacier (rice + lag)
7. Grand Teton (noted + grant)
8. Crater Lake (tracker + ale)
9. Carlsbad Caverns (crave + bland + scars)
10. Big Bend (bed + Bing)

Puzzles on page 71

SYNANAGRAMS

1. Poodle (pod + Leo)
2. Samoyed (yam + dose)
3. English Sheepdog (gelding + hopes + she)
4. Siamese (aim + sees)
5. Greyhound (rough + deny)
6. Bullmastiff (flub + film + sat)
7. Irish Setter (hitters + sire)
8. Great Dane (gander + eat)
9. Abyssinian (any + bias + sin)
10. Pomeranian (nap + romaine)

Puzzles on page 72

Incomplete Alphabet Messages   (Kid-Friendly Bonus)   6

1. DOG gone
2. ACTING out
3. DEARLY departed
4. TWICE removed (or shy)
5. SOUND off
6. RUN away (or down/out)
7. DOUBLE crossed
8. SLOWING down
9. TURN left (or off/away/down/loose)
10. WILDCAT strike

Puzzles on page 73

INDEX TO PUZZLES

bonus puzzles
  Incomplete Alphabet
    Messages (for adults), 73
  Name Shuffles (for kids), 48
  Sam, Dan & Ron Are Hiding
    (for kids), 62
Celebrities, 55–62
  Actors, 58–59
  Athletes, 60–61
  Sam, Dan & Ron Are
    Hiding, 62
  Singers, 56–57
Hidden Things, 63–66
  Hidden Authors, 66
  Hidden Automobile Models,
    65
  Hidden Math Words, 64
kid-friendly bonuses
  Name Shuffles, 48
  Sam, Dan & Ron Are
    Hiding, 62
Quick Word Puzzles, 7–26
  Add-a-Letter, 21–22
  Add-On Words, 25–26
  Drop Letters, 23–24
  Holiday Season Letter
    Zappers, 17–18
  J Puzzles, 10

  K Puzzles, 12
  Movies–the 1980s, 13–14
  Non-Repeaters, 15–16
  Q Puzzles, 8
  Words of the Presidents,
    19–20
  X Puzzles, 11
  Z Puzzles, 9
Something in Common, 27–48
  Names & Places, 41–47
  Name Shuffles, 48–49
  Miscellany, 29–34
  Same-Size Words, 35–40
Special Days, 49–54
  Columbus Day, 54
  Independence Day, 52
  Labor Day, 53
  St. Patrick's Day, 51
  Valentine's Day, 50
Synanagrams, 67–73
  Chemical Elements, 69
  Dog & Cat Breeds, 72
  National Parks, 71
  Incomplete Alphabet
    Messages, 73
  Professional Sports Teams, 70
  States & Provinces in North
    America, 68

INDEX TO ANSWERS

answers, 75–92
bonus puzzles
  Incomplete Alphabet
    Messages (for adults), 92
  Name Shuffles (for kids), 83
  Sam, Dan & Ron Are Hiding
    (for kids), 87
Celebrities, 86
  Actors, 86
  Athletes, 87
  Sam, Dan & Ron Are
    Hiding, 87
  Singers, 86
Hidden Things, 88–89
  Hidden Authors, 89
  Hidden Automobile Models,
    88
  Hidden Math Words, 88
kid-friendly bonuses
  Name Shuffles, 83
  Sam, Dan & Ron Are
    Hiding, 87
Quick Word Puzzles, 76–80
  Add-a-Letter, 79
  Add-On Words, 80
  Drop Letters, 80
  Holiday Season Letter
    Zappers, 78

J Puzzles, 76
K Puzzles, 77
Movies–the 1980s, 77
Non-Repeaters, 78
Q Puzzles, 76
Words of the Presidents, 79
X Puzzles, 76
Z Puzzles, 76
Something in Common, 81–82
  Names & Places, 83
  Name Shuffles, 83
  Miscellany, 81
  Same-Size Words, 82
Special Days, 84–85
  Columbus Day, 85
  Independence Day, 85
  Labor Day, 84
  St. Patrick's Day, 84
  Valentine's Day, 84
Synanagrams, 90–91
  Chemical Elements, 90
  Dog & Cat Breeds, 92
  National Parks, 91
  Incomplete Alphabet
    Messages, 92
  Professional Sports Teams, 91
  States & Provinces in North
    America, 90

WHAT IS MENSA?

Mensa
The High IQ Society

Mensa is the international society for people with a high IQ. We have more than 100,000 members in over 40 countries worldwide.

The society's aims are:

- to identify and foster human intelligence for the benefit of humanity;
- to encourage research in the nature, characteristics, and uses of intelligence;
- to provide a stimulating intellectual and social environment for its members.

Anyone with an IQ score in the top two percent of the population is eligible to become a member of Mensa–are you the "one in 50" we've been looking for?

Mensa membership offers an excellent range of benefits:

- Networking and social activities nationally and around the world;
- Special Interest Groups (hundreds of chances to pursue your hobbies and interests–from art to zoology!);
- Monthly International Journal, national magazines, and regional newsletters;

- Local meetings—from game challenges to food and drink;
- National and international weekend gatherings and conferences;
- Intellectually stimulating lectures and seminars;
- Access to the worldwide SIGHT network for travelers and hosts.

For more information about Mensa International: www.mensa.org

MENSA INTERNATIONAL
15 The Ivories
6–8 Northampton Street
Islington, London N1 2HY
United Kingdom

For more information about American Mensa:
www.us.mensa.org
Telephone: 1–800–66MENSA
American Mensa Ltd.
1229 Corporate Drive West
Arlington, TX 76006-6103 USA

For more information about British Mensa
(UK and Ireland):
www.mensa.org.uk
Telephone: +44 (0) 1902 772771
E-mail: enquiries@mensa.org.uk
British Mensa Ltd.
St. John's House
St. John's Square
Wolverhampton WV2 4AH
United Kingdom

For more information about Australian Mensa:
www.au.mensa.org
Telephone: +61 1902 260 594
E-mail: info@au.mensa.org
Australian Mensa Inc.
PO Box 212
Darlington WA 6070 Australia